EASY HOME
IMPROVEMENTS

your
home office

EASY HOME IMPROVEMENTS

your home office

STEWART WALTON

LEBHAR-FRIEDMAN BOOKS

New York • Chicago • Los Angeles • London • Paris • Tokyo

Lebhar-Friedman Books
425 Park Avenue
New York, NY 10022

Published by Lebhar-Friedman Books
Lebhar-Friedman Books is a company of Lebhar-Friedman, Inc.

Printed and bound in China by Excel Printing.
Originated in Singapore by Pica.

Library of Congress Cataloging-in-Publication Data
on file at the Library of Congress.

ISBN: 0-86730-836-2

Project Editor Guy Croton
Designer Glen Wilkins
Editorial Coordinator Caroline Watson
Photographer Alistair Hughes
Managing Editor Antonia Cunningham
Managing Art Editor Phil Gilderdale
Editorial Director Ellen Dupont
Art Director Dave Goodman
Production Amanda Mackie

Front cover photography: **Tim Street-Porter (Josh Schweitzer)**
Back cover photography: **Alistair Hughes**

Visit our Web site at lfbooks.com

Note

contents

Introduction   6

Chapter 1: The room

Making a Venetian blind valance   10

Laying a foam-backed carpet   16

Making a home-office screen   22

Building an office step stool   32

Chapter 2: Shelving

Making a book-ended shelf   42

Making a tall bookcase   50

Creating desktop shelving   58

Chapter 3: The desk

Making a magazine organizer   70

Making a desk tidy   76

Making a mail box   84

Making a printer/CPU trolley   92

Building a computer desk   100

Glossary   110

Index   111

introduction

As communications become increasingly advanced, more and more people are working at home. Additionally, with the ubiquitous and unstoppable rise of the PC, even those who still travel to an office every day need a space at home where they can work or play on their personal computer. Once every large home incorporated a study—now, every home, whatever its size, needs a home office.

Offices are traditionally functional, often dull rooms that are designed with the minimum of fuss and the maximum of productivity in mind. In the past, many corporate office designers apparently believed that people work best in gray, drab surroundings with minimal distractions. They were wrong. Research shows that people actually respond better in their working environment to cheerful colors and well-designed, aesthetically pleasing furnishings. You might not be able to persuade your boss at work that it is time for a complete office makeover, but when it comes to your own home-working space, the choice of decor and furnishings is of course entirely up to you.

This book can help you make the most of your home office—or whatever space you have at home for working on the computer, dealing with correspondence, and paying bills. It is packed with practical projects that range from laying a carpet (pages 16–21) to building a computer printer/CPU trolley (pages 92–99) or an entire desktop shelving unit (pages 58–67).

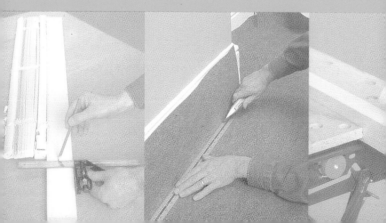

There are projects designed both to enhance and utilize the full potential of the office space—like the Venetian blind valance on pages 10–15 and the office step stool on pages 32–39. Others are based on the desk—the heart of any office—and how to get the most from it. In addition to the desktop shelving unit and printer/CPU trolley mentioned earlier, these other projects include a neat and highly economical computer desk and a desktop "tidy" for small storage solutions. Additionally, a chapter of projects designed with office storage in mind features a stylish bookcase (pages 50–57) and a book-ended shelf, among others.

Although accurate measurements and dimensions are supplied to assist with the construction of every project, in some cases there is no reason why you should not scale them proportionally up or down from the existing measurements to suit your own specific space requirements. No special skills are required to construct the projects to a reasonable standard, although a basic proficiency in woodworking and joinery would be a definite advantage.

The main considerations when building these projects is that you follow all the instructions carefully, be patient and take your time, ask for assistance when necessary, and use good quality tools and materials. Full guidance is given as to the level of difficulty of an individual project, roughly how long it will take to make, and what you will need, but in the end only you can be the judge of what exactly to use and how well your work is likely to turn out.

I hope you find these projects as enjoyable and fulfilling to make as I did in preparing them for this book.

Stewart Walton

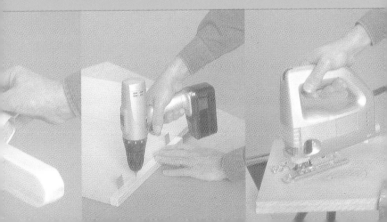

chapter 1

The room

1. Making a Venetian blind valance

2. Laying a foam-backed carpet

3. Making a home-office screen

4. Building an office step stool

making a Venetian blind valance

Venetian blinds work well with office windows, as they are functional, versatile, and easier to clean than drapes. They are also one of the most attractive and effective means of adjusting the amount of light you let into your room. However, the fixing brackets are not always particularly attractive and can be covered up with this easy-to-make wooden valance. Remember, there are lots of different types of blinds, so be sure to follow the manufacturer's instructions when fitting your blind and adapt these to the following project guidance.

Materials (all lumber is softwood unless otherwise stated)

1 piece of 60 in. x 2½ x ¾ in. lumber • 1 piece of 72 in. mahogany • Venetian blind • 3 right-angled metal brackets • No. 6 (1½ in.) screws • Panel pins

Tools

Workbench • Tape measure • Set-square/combination square • Miter saw • Carpenter's pencil • Power drill with pilot hole, screw, and ½ in. bits • Hammer • Straightedge/rule • Spirit level

Skill level

Intermediate

Time

4 hours

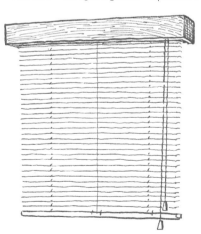

Easy home improvements

1. Fix the end brackets to your Venetian blind, following the manufacturer's instructions. Place the blind on a piece of scrap plywood on top of your workbench. Take the piece of 2½ x ¾ in. lumber. This will form the valance shelf that will be attached to the wall above your blind and window, and will support the valance box. Mark it with a pencil and set-square to a length that is ½ in. greater at each end than the length of your blind.

2. Cut the piece of 2½ x ¾ in. lumber to the required length. Using a rule and pencil, measure and mark the positions of the three brackets with which your valance shelf will be attached to the wall. Two of these should be positioned 3 in. in from each end of the valance shelf, with the third centered between them. Screw the brackets to the lumber.

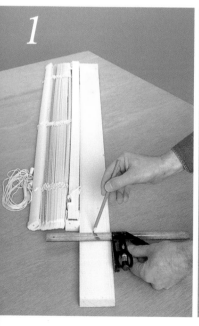

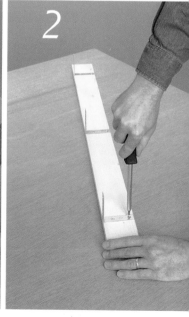

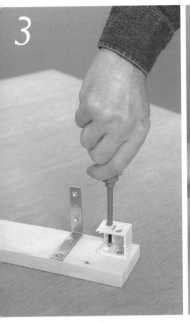

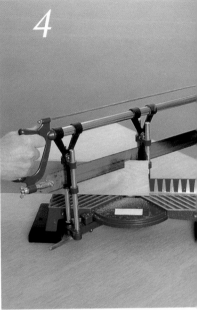

3 Remove the plastic fixing brackets from the end of the Venetian blind and mark where they need to be positioned at the ends of the valance shelf. The brackets should be positioned ½ in. in from the back edge of the valance shelf (which will be attached to the wall), and the same distance in from the ends of the shelf. Screw the plastic blind brackets to the valance shelf.

4 Measure and cut out the four mahogany pieces that make up the box that fits over the valance shelf. The overall dimensions of the valance box should be ¼ in. greater than those of the shelf it will fit over, to allow it to slide into place once the shelf has been fixed to the wall. Use a miter saw to cut 45-degree miters, for neat, tight joints at each end of the box.

5 Position the pieces of the valance box together on the workbench. Hammer panel pins part-way through each piece to facilitate assembling the box. Use five or six pins along the front edge of the box and two in each end. Ensure they are evenly spaced. Assemble the valance box, by gluing sparingly along each joint and then hammering in the pins. Begin by attaching the end pieces to the top of the box and then add the long front piece that will cover the top of the Venetian blind. Once you have hammered all the pins in, use a nail-punch and hammer to tap their heads a little farther into the wood.

6 Offer up the valance shelf and attached brackets to the wall above your window. Measure and mark the positions of the fixing brackets, using a rule, spirit level, and pencil.

7   Mark and drill pilot holes to the width of a No. 6 (1½ in.) screw into the walls through the fixing holes of the brackets. Insert wallplugs. Attach the Venetian blind shelf and brackets to the wall using No. 6 (1½ in.) screws and an electric screwdriver.

8   Secure the Venetian blind in place in its plastic brackets that were attached to the valance shelf in step 3. Slide the valance box into position over the valance shelf. Once you are satisfied with the fit of the blind and the valance box over it, remove the valance box and fill, sand, and decorate it as you wish.

laying a
foam-backed carpet

Carpeting your home office is an efficient and attractive flooring option. As long as you don't use synthetic material, carpet will help to reduce the amount of static electricity created by your computer and other electrical equipment, thus reducing the build-up of dust. Carpet also helps to keep the room warm, and if your office is small, you can use cheap remnants and cut down on costs. You can also cheer up the office by using a bright color, if you so wish. However, please note that this method is suitable only for small areas and that larger areas will usually require underlay and a different method for attaching the carpet.

Materials
Woven carpet • Double-sided adhesive tape

Tools
Heavy-duty craft knife and spare blades • Long, metal straightedge • Tape measure • Bolster or blunt chisel • Felt-tip pen or marker

Skill level
Beginner

Time
4 hours

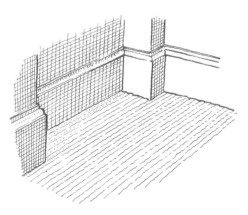

1 Ensure that the floor to be carpeted is sound, even, and free of dust. If you are using underlay, this should be put down first, following the manufacturer's instructions. Otherwise, spread newspaper or plain brown paper prior to laying your carpet. Unroll your carpet and butt it roughly up to the skirting boards or bottoms of the walls, ensuring that you allow enough of an overlap on the unrolled edge to allow the carpet to run into any farther recesses that require a longer length. Measure and draw a pen line on the back of the carpet, indicating the line of cut you need to make to the wall.

2 Use a heavy-duty craft knife to cut through the carpet from its underside along the line that you drew in step 1. Ensure that you do not allow the blade to score through the topside of the carpet underneath, as you make your cut into the underside of the folded-over excess.

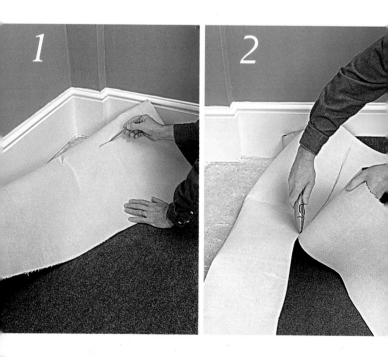

3 Butt your cut edge neatly and precisely up to the back wall. Then make a "release" cut at the exterior corner of any recess or protruding corner (as shown), ensuring that you do not cut too far into the carpet at the corner of the wall where it meets the floor.

4 Use a bolster or blunt chisel to push the carpet right up flush against the back wall, so that it almost nudges underneath the edge of any skirting board. Be careful not to damage the edge of the carpet with the bolster.

Helpful hints

You will need lots of new, sharp blades for your craft knife, as carpet fabric always blunts blades very quickly. A blunt blade is ineffective and dangerous.

5 Press a long, metal straightedge hard-up against the pushed-in edge of the carpet where it meets the wall or skirting board. Take your heavy-duty craft knife and cut along the edge of the metal rule, scoring firmly through the entire thickness of the carpet. Ensure that your cut line is straight and true and avoid leaving any straggling, uncut threads.

6 Repeat the process described in step 3 on the first interior corner of the recess. First make a release cut on the rear interior corner, and then another at the exterior corner where the recess ends, as shown. Trim off the excess carpet and repeat step 5 to cut the edge of the carpet neatly along the back wall in the recess.

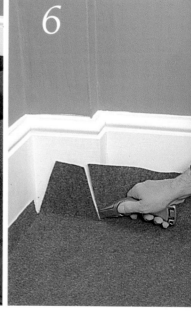

7 Make the final release cut at the last interior corner of the recess, where the end of the recess re-joins the side wall. Leave your excess carpet up against the skirting board to be trimmed away later, once you are sure of the overall fit into the corner. Use a bolster or blunt chisel in the method described in step 4 to press the carpet up tight against the last edge of the recess, again almost nudging the carpet underneath any skirting board. Trim off the excess piece of carpet.

8 Lay double-sided adhesive tape along the edges of the floor, where it meets the walls. Peel off the backing of the tape and press the carpet firmly down onto the exposed, sticky side. Use your hands and feet to smooth out any lumps along the edge of the carpet and trim any rough edges as necessary.

making a
home-office screen

A screen is a useful item in your home office. If you share your home office with someone else, there may be times when you need a little privacy, or it can screen off your work station if it is in a room used for other things, such as your living room. Moreover, as it is temporary and portable, it can be stored away out of sight when it is not in use. This wooden and canvas project is straightforward and rewarding to construct.

Materials (all lumber is softwood unless otherwise stated)

Panel uprights: Six pieces of PAR lumber measuring
2 x 1½ x 60 in.

Dowel cross pieces: Six pieces of dowel measuring
¾ x 19 in.

Roll of canvas measuring 18 x 200 in. • Six brass hinges • No. 8 (2 in.) brass screws and screw cups • Brass, round-headed panel pins • Double-sided adhesive tape

Tools

Workbench • Tape measure • Combination square • Tenon saw • Miter saw • Pencil • Power drill with pilot hole, screw, and ⅛-in. bits • Hammer • Bradawl • Rule • Abrasive paper/sanding block • Brush

Skill level

Intermediate

Time

4 hours

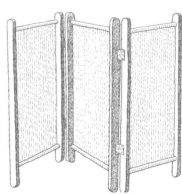

Easy home improvements

1 Measure and cut out all the pieces to the dimensions given in the list of materials. Take each of the six pieces of PAR lumber measuring 2 x 1½ in. in turn, and use a combination square and pencil to mark off 45-degree angles ½ in. in from each edge at the end of each piece of lumber. These pieces will make up the six panel uprights, and need to have cut and rounded-off ends to prevent them splintering when the completed screen is moved around on the floor.

2 Clamp each panel upright in turn horizontally to the workbench and use a tenon saw to make the angled cuts at each end. Follow your pencil guidelines carefully and ensure that the cuts are straight.

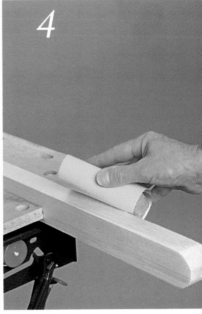

3 Clamp each panel upright in turn vertically into the workbench. Use a sanding block and paper to smooth off the ends that you cut in step 2. Use medium-grade abrasive paper first, and then finish off with fine-grade paper to get a nice, smooth finish.

4 Return each of the uprights to a horizontal position in the workbench and sand along all sides and edges for a smooth, graded finish all over. Again, start off with medium-grade abrasive paper over a block and then use fine paper to finish off. Once you have finished sanding all six uprights, brush everything off thoroughly.

5 Use a rule, set-square, and pencil to mark a central point 3 in. in from the ends of each upright. This marks where the dowel cross pieces will be secured into the uprights. The three canvas sections will be suspended from the dowel cross pieces, which connect the six uprights and complete the frames of the screen panels. Mark the uprights in pairs, to ensure the accurate and consistent positioning of the fixing marks.

6 Once you have marked out all the positions of the dowel cross pieces on the panel uprights in pencil, use a bradawl to make a small "siting" hole for the point of the big drill-bit you will use to drill out the holes. This will help secure the drill-bit in the wood and will ensure accurately sited holes for the ends of the dowel cross pieces.

7 Attach a piece of masking tape to a ⅞-in. drill-bit to mark
the depth to which you want to drill each hole. Hold the
drill-bit across the width of one of the uprights and align
it in such a position that the tip of the drill-bit will not
pierce the back side of the upright as it makes the hole.
The tape should be attached to mark a point on the drill-
bit that will prevent the head of the bit bursting through
the back sides of the uprights.

8 Clamp each upright into the workbench in turn and use
the taped drill-bit to make the holes for the dowel cross
pieces. Hold a square in position as you drill the holes,
to ensure that you keep the drill-bit straight and the
holes are each drilled straight and vertically. Ensure that
you do not allow the drill-bit to penetrate the wood any
deeper than the tape marker denotes.

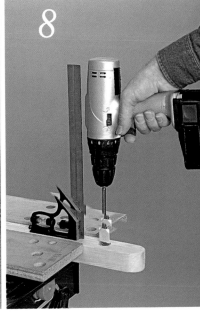

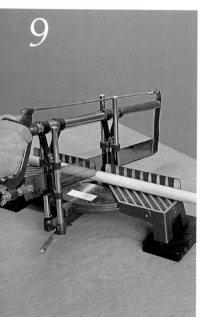

9   Cut each of the dowel cross pieces to length on a miter saw. They should measure 19 in. in total, allowing for the width of the canvas sections and the ½ in. at each end of the dowel that will be plugged in to the panel uprights. Smooth off the cut ends with abrasive paper.

10 Place a dowel cross piece in position in one of the holes in the panel uprights. Use a pencil and combination square to transfer the positions of the central points of the dowels onto the back sides of the panel uprights. These pencil marks show the positions of the pilot screw holes that you will need to drill through the backs of the uprights and into the dowel pieces in order to secure them properly.

1 Using a combination square to ensure your joints are straight, drill from above through the backs of the panel uprights and into the ends of the dowel cross pieces, top and bottom. Repeat the process for all the panel uprights and all the dowel cross pieces.

2 Squeeze wood glue into each of the dowel holes on all six of the panel uprights. Be careful not to use too much, to avoid excess glue spilling over the wood. If it does spill, wipe it off promptly using a damp cloth.

Helpful hints

Use a strip of double-sided tape to help secure the entire width of the canvas to the dowel cross piece before you hammer in the tacks.

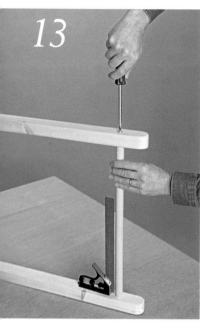

13 Use 2 in. No. 8 brass screws and screw cups to attach each of the dowel cross pieces to the panel uprights. Be sure your joints are properly squared-up, using a combination square, before you begin screwing.

14 Take each of the three complete panel frames in turn and begin attaching the screen canvas on the workbench. Wrap the end of the canvas tightly around the top dowel cross piece using tape to secure it in place, and then unroll the canvas along the full length of the panel frame. Use a hammer and five evenly spaced tacks to secure the canvas to the top dowel cross piece. Cut the canvas to the correct length, ensuring it is taut and square in the panel frame, and secure its bottom edge to the bottom dowel cross piece. Repeat the whole process with the other two panel frames.

5 Measure and mark the positions of the hinges for attaching the three canvas panels together. Space them evenly on the panel uprights, 12 in. from each end, top, and bottom. Attach the hinges to the panel uprights, using brass screws. Begin with the center panel first, attaching one hinge to the front-left edge of one panel upright and the other hinge to the back-right edge of the other upright, in order to effect an "accordion" fold in the screen as a whole.

6 Stand the three panels upright in order to attach them to one another with the hinges. Ensure that the panels are correctly aligned and completely square with one another before joining them together. Check that your accordion-fold effect works correctly across the three panels before securing them all together.

building an
office step stool

If you have a small home office, you might have maximized the available space by installing high-level shelves on the walls. If that is the case, then an office step stool will be perfect for assisting you in reaching those awkward, out-of-the-way storage areas. It is cheaper to make, more attractive and less cumbersome than a full-sized set of steps, and will also be useful in other areas of the home.

Materials (all lumber is softwood unless otherwise stated)

Sides: 2 pieces of MDF ¾ x 25 x 15 in.
Steps: 2 pieces of MDF ¾ x 6¾ x 14½ in.
Front and back cross braces: 3 pieces of beech ¾ x 16 x 2½ in. • No. 6 (1½ in.) brass screws and screw cups • 1 in. panel pins • Small tin of matte varnish or wax polish

Tools

Workbench • Jigsaw • Tenon saw • Hammer • Tape measure • Combination square • Carpenter's pencil • Power drill with pilot hole, screw, ⅛ in., and ⅙ in. bits • Rule • Paint brush • Fine- and medium-grade abrasive paper and block

Skill level

Intermediate

Time

4 hours

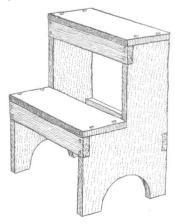

1 Take one of the side pieces and mark out the semi-circular recess to be cut at its bottom and the rectangle of board that needs to be removed to accommodate the lower step. The semi-circle should be drawn with a pencil and compass around a line marked down the center of the side piece, to a radius of 5 in. The rectangle to be cut out of the side piece should measure 10 in. deep by 7½ in. wide from the top left-hand corner of the side piece. Shade the areas to be cut out. Mark the position for the back cross brace, 7 in. up from the bottom edge of the side piece.

2 Pin the two side pieces together ready for cutting out the rectangle and semi-circular recesses. Be careful to hammer the 1 in. pins only through the shaded areas, which denote the excess wood to be cut out.

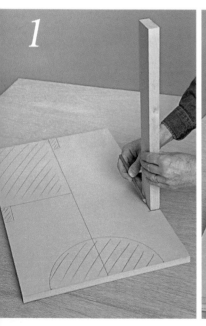

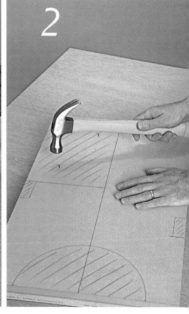

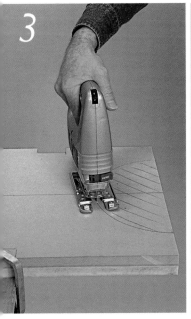

3 Clamp the two pinned side pieces onto a workbench. Use a jigsaw to cut out the semi-circular recesses that you marked out in step 1. Next, clamp the two pinned side pieces vertically in the jaws of the workbench, with the marked-out rectangular section facing upward. Use a tenon saw to cut out the rectangle from both side pieces. Sand off and smooth any rough edges or splinters.

4 When you have finished cutting out the rectangular section, take one of the cross brace pieces and hold it up to one of the side pieces. Use a pencil to mark the position of the end of the lower cross brace at the outside, bottom edge of the rectangle that you cut out in step 3 (as shown). Repeat the process on the other side piece and again for the two ends of the top cross brace. In the latter case, the rebates should be marked at the top, front edge of the rectangle that you cut out in step 3.

5 Following the guidelines you marked in step 4, use a tenon saw to cut out the rebates for the two front cross braces.

6 Thoroughly sand the cut-out rebates and rectangular section edges using medium-grade abrasive paper wrapped around a sanding block or an old wood offcut. Smooth off with fine-grade abrasive paper.

Helpful hints

When cutting out rebates in wood, always cut slightly "tight" —that is, fractionally inside your guidelines. It is easier to sand a rebate to the right size than to correct one that is too big.

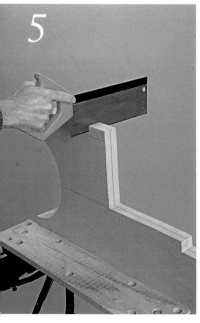

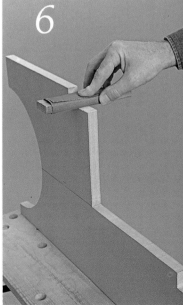

7 When you have completed the cutting and sanding of the four rebates, hold the cross braces up to the side pieces to ensure that they fit tightly and squarely into the rebates. At this stage, make any adjustments to ensure sound joints. This will make assembly and finishing work easier to complete later on.

8 Measure and mark two evenly spaced fixing holes in each end of both cross braces. Use a ⅛ in. drill-bit to drill clearance holes at each marked point. Place a piece of scrap wood under the cross braces as you drill, to avoid making holes in your workbench.

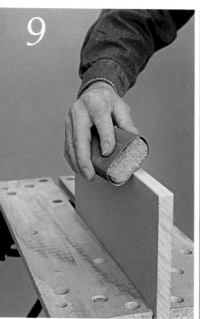

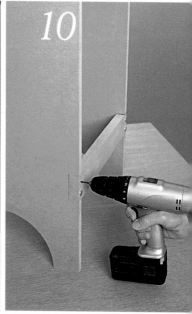

9   Take the two step pieces and clamp them into the
    workbench, one after the other. Use a sanding block
    and abrasive paper to sand off all rough edges and the
    surfaces. Begin with medium-grade paper and then use
    fine-grade to finish off.

10 Begin assembling the office step stool by fixing the
    back cross brace to the two side pieces. Use a ⅛ in. drill
    bit to drill reciprocal pilot holes into the backs of the
    side pieces through the cross brace clearance holes you
    drilled in step 8. Secure the back cross brace using
    No. 6 (1½ in.) brass screws and screw cups to recess
    the screwheads and serve as a decorative feature.

11 Next, use the same method as decribed in step 10 to attach the two steps and two front cross braces to the side pieces of the unit. Again, use brass screws recessed in screw cups to enhance the look of the steps. You might find it easier to use a hand-held screwdriver rather than a power drill.

12 Once the office step stool has been fully assembled, fill and sand the unit as necessary. Complete the project by applying two coats of matte varnish. Alternatively, wax and polish the unit to a stylish finish.

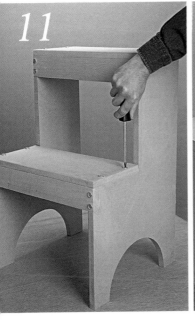

chapter 2

Shelving

1. Making a book-ended shelf
2. Making a tall bookcase
3. Creating desktop shelving

making a
book-ended shelf

You can never have too many shelves in an office—there is always a multitude of computer discs, books, files, and papers that need storing away. This small shelf is particularly useful because the built-in bookends prevent books and CDs from falling sideways. It is big enough to hold the items you are constantly reaching for, yet small enough not to take up too much space above, or on, your desk.

Materials

Shelf: 1 piece of lightweight hardwood 1¼ x 7½ x 32 in.
Sides: 2 pieces of lightweight hardwood 1¼ x 7½ x 11¼ in.
Shelf edging: cut from length of mahogany ¼ x 1¼ in. x 7 ft.
2 mirror-style brass fixing brackets • No. 6 (1½ in.) screws •
Wood glue • Wood filler • Masking tape

Tools

Workbench • Tenon saw • Tape measure • Rule • Craft knife •
Filling knife • Combination square • Carpenter's pencil • Power drill with screw, countersinking, ⅛ in., and ⅛ in. bits • Hand screwdriver • Abrasive paper/sanding block

Skill level

Beginner

Time

4 hours

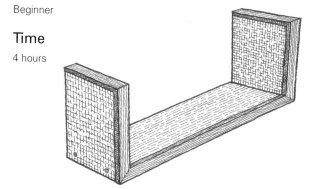

1 Measure and cut all the pieces to the dimensions given in the list of materials. Hold both the side pieces up to the shelf and ensure that their bottoms are cut absolutely straight to enable a completely square joint with the shelf at both ends. Use a combination square to satisfy yourself that the joints will be square.

2 Still holding the shelf sides in position, use a pencil to draw a fixing guideline across the width of the shelf at both ends on its underside. Next, mark three evenly spaced clearance fixing holes in the center of the pencil guidelines. These show the positions of the screws that will attach the sides to the shelf.

3 Hold the two side pieces tightly up against each other on the workbench and drill their fixing holes. Use a ⅛ in. drill-bit to drill the clearance holes in the outsides of the shelf sides, ensuring that they are evenly spaced and positioned in precisely the same places on each side piece. When you have finished drilling, countersink the holes.

4 Hold each of the side pieces up in turn to the shelf and use a smaller, ⅛ in. drill-bit to drill reciprocal pilot holes into the ends of the shelf, through the clearance holes you drilled in the side pieces in step 3. Ensure that all your marks line up accurately before drilling the holes.

5 Apply wood glue sparingly to the fixing end of each side piece. This will help strengthen the joints that you are about to make with screws. Be careful not to use too much glue and wipe off any excess with a damp cloth. Attach the side pieces to the shelf using No. 6 (1½ in.) screws.

6 Once you have assembled the basic "U"-shape of the shelf unit, it is time to attach the mahogany shelf facings. Cut a strip of mahogany to a length slightly greater than that of the shelf and its attached sides. Hold it in position along the side of the shelf. Use a pencil and rule to mark the positions of 45-degree miter joints at the corners where the shelf joins the two side pieces.

7 Use a miter saw to cut 45-degree miter joints into each end of the mahogany strip. Make precise cuts and then sand off any rough edges to the miters using fine abrasive paper and a block.

8 Repeat the process described in steps 6 and 7 to prepare the mitered mahogany edgings for the front edges of the two side pieces. First miter the joints meeting the mahogany edging to be attached to the front of the shelf. Then, hold the side edging pieces in position and carefully mark off straight cuts across their top edges, ensuring that these are flush with the tops of the side pieces.

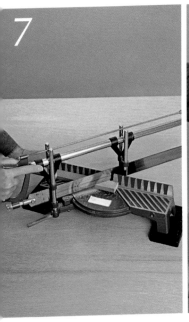

9   Once you are satisfied with the lengths and miter joints of the mahogany edging pieces, attach them to the front edges of the unit using wood glue. Apply the glue sparingly and wipe off any excess immediately with a damp cloth. Use strips of masking tape to hold the mahogany edgings in place as the glue dries.

10   Use a ⅛ in. drill-bit to drill fixing holes for the two brackets to attach the shelf unit to the wall. These should be drilled into the top back edges of the sides.

Helpful hints

If you can find it, use low-tack masking tape to hold the mahogany edgings in place. This is less likely to leave a sticky residue behind than standard masking tape.

1 Complete the shelf unit by thoroughly filling all the screw holes and any obvious gaps in the joints with wood filler and a flexible filling knife. Wait for the filler to dry, and then sand it off to a smooth finish.

2 Finally, attach the shelf fixing brackets to the sides, following any manufacturer's instructions supplied with the brackets. Use a hand-held screwdriver rather than a power drill, to ensure accuracy in your screwing and to avoid damaging the wood of the shelf. The shelf unit is now ready to be attached to the wall.

11

12

making a
tall bookcase

Bookcases are generally not too expensive to buy, but it is often difficult to find one that is the right size or shape and that fits in with the other furniture in your office. A good solution is to make your own, and this project can be easily adapted to fit your particular needs. It is inexpensive and straightforward to construct, requiring only a little woodworking and joining skills. The bare wood will look attractive in most office settings, or you can varnish or paint it to your taste.

Materials

Back: 1 piece of MDF 1 x 16 x 36 in.

Sides: 2 pieces of MDF 1 x 12 x 36 in.

Shelves: 3 pieces of MDF 1 x 10 x 16 in.

Shelf facings: 3 pieces of oak ½ x 2 x 16 in.

Four castors • No. 6 (1½ in.) screws • Wood glue

Tools

Workbench • Tenon saw • Tape measure • Rule • Combination square • Carpenter's pencil • Power drill with screw, countersinking, ⅛ in., and ⅛ in. bits • Abrasive paper/block • Masking tape

Skill level

Intermediate

Time

4 hours

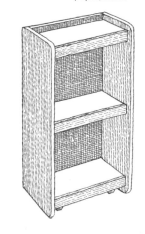

Easy home improvements

1. Measure and cut all the pieces to the dimensions given in the list of materials. Using an egg-cup as a guide—or anything with a similarly sized round edge—draw rounded corners on both the front top and bottom corners of the two side pieces. Use a pencil to shade the areas of wood to be cut away.

2. Clamp each side piece in turn into the workbench. Use a tenon saw to cut the four corners at a 45-degree angle across the tops of the rounded guidelines you marked in step 1. Be sure to stay slightly shy of your pencil marks, keeping the saw-blade on the waste-wood side. Next, take a sanding block or piece of scrap wood and some medium-grade abrasive paper. Sand all four corners into smooth curves, keeping your hand at right-angles to the wood as you sand across it.

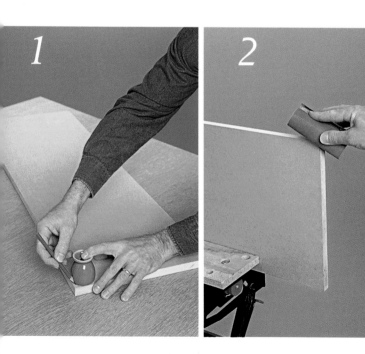

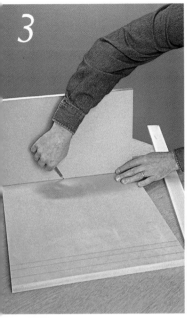

3 Take the back piece and lay it flat on the workbench. Hold up each of the three shelf pieces in turn and mark their positions on the back piece, using a pencil to draw along the top and bottom edges of each shelf. The top shelf should be positioned 1 in. down from the top edge of the back piece. The bottom shelf should be positioned 3 in. up from the bottom edge. The middle shelf should be positioned equidistant between the top and bottom shelves.

4 Lay the side pieces next to the back piece on the workbench. Make sure that they butt tightly together, keeping them square, and ensure that the top edges of all pieces are level with each other. Then use a combination square, rule, and pencil to transfer the shelf positions from the back piece onto the two sides.

Easy home improvements

5   Mark out the positions for screw-fixing clearance holes
on the back piece and two sides of the unit. Each shelf
will require three screws to attach to the back piece
and three to attach to each side, so you need to drill
nine clearance holes for each shelf. Mark the positions
of the holes centrally in your pencil guidelines and
ensure that they are evenly spaced. Drill the clearance
holes using a ⅛ in. drill-bit. Place a piece of old scrap
wood under the pieces as you drill, to prevent making
holes in your workbench. Countersink all the clearance
holes from the exteriors of the sides and back piece.

6   Hold up each of the shelves to the back piece, set them
square to one another, and drill reciprocal, smaller pilot
holes into the backs of the shelves through each of the
clearance holes using a ⅛ in. drill-bit.

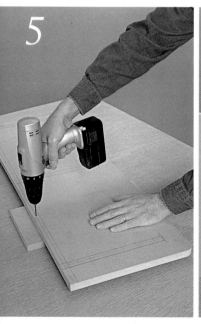

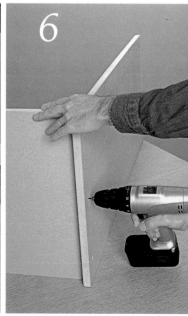

7 Use No. 6 (1½ in.) screws and wood glue to attach each of the shelves to the back piece. Then set the back piece and shelves on their side on the workbench and prepare to attach the two side pieces. Repeat the process described in step 6, drilling smaller, reciprocal pilot holes into the sides of the shelves through the side pieces' clearance holes. Attach each of the side pieces to the unit using the same method described above. Be sure that all joints are square and secure.

8 The next stage is to prepare and attach the three shelf facings. To measure the precise size for each of the facings, hold up the pieces to the unit and mark them off to a width slightly greater than that of the shelves. Butt the pieces fully up against the sides of the bookcase. Cut each facing squarely to size using a tenon saw.

9 To attach the shelf facings, first apply wood glue to the front edges of each of the shelves. Gently press the facings onto the glued surfaces. The facings should hang down from the top edge of each shelf and should not overlap above the shelf. Once each facing is in position, wipe away any excess glue with a damp cloth. Secure the facings in place with strips of masking tape. When the glue is fully dry, remove the masking tape.

10 Use wood filler and a flexible filling knife to fill the countersunk clearance screw holes. Lightly smooth over the holes with the filler knife. Do not worry about filling perfectly, as sanding will correct any mistakes once the filler is dry. Also fill any loose joints or other gaps in the unit.

1 Use a sanding block and abrasive paper to rub down any areas that have been filled. Next, cut four 3 x 3 in. squares of offcut MDF board to use as plinths for the castors that attach to the base of the bookcase. Turn the unit upside down on the workbench and place each of the four MDF plinths snugly into each corner. Drill four clearance holes into the corners of each plinth and attach them with No. 6 (1½ in.) screws.

2 Fix the four castors to the base of the unit, following the manufacturer's instructions. Paint or varnish the finished bookcase as you wish.

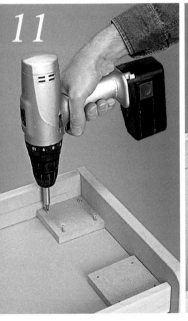

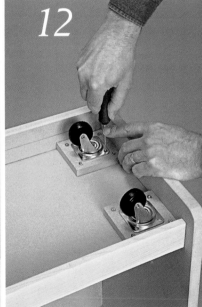

creating
desktop shelving

Many desks offer only a straightforward, plain work-surface without any accompanying storage space beyond a couple of drawers. When space is at a premium, as it so often is in a home office, you might need something a little more versatile, like this ingenious desktop shelving unit.

Materials

Back: 1 piece of MDF ¾ x 27 x 40¾ in. • **Top shelf:** 1 piece of MDF ¾ x 13 x 40¾ in. • **Bottom shelf:** 1 piece of MDF ¾ x 12 x 12¾ in. • **Small side shelves:** 2 pieces of MDF ¾ x 6 x 6 in. • **Top shelf upright divider:** 1 piece of MDF ¾ x 12 x 8¼ in.• **Bottom shelf upright divider:** 1 piece of MDF ¾ x 12 x 14 in. • **Left-hand uprights:** 2 pieces of MDF ¾ x 6 x 6 in. • **Right-hand uprights:** 2 pieces of MDF ¾ x 18 x 6 in. • No. 6 (1½ in.) screws • Wood glue

Tools

Workbench • Jigsaw • Tape measure • Combination square • Carpenter's pencil • Power drill with pilot hole, screw, countersinking, ⅛ in., and ⅛ in. bits • Hammer • Rule • Abrasive paper/sanding block

Skill level

Advanced

Time

8 hours

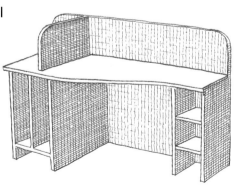

Easy home improvements

1. Hold the uprights, dividers, and shelves up to the back piece in turn and mark out their positions. Start with the uprights that are positioned at each end of the unit. Draw their positions flush with the ends and bottom edge of the back piece. Next, the position of the top shelf should be drawn across the width of the back piece, 8¼ in. down from its top edge. The bottom shelf should be positioned 14 in. below the top shelf, its left-hand edge flush with the left-hand upright. Once you have marked the positions of the two main shelves, draw the positions of the interior uprights at their innermost edges. Finally, mark the positions of the two small, right-hand side shelves, 15 in. and 21 in. down from the top edge of the back piece.

2. Use a small plate or saucer to draw round corners on the top two corners of the back piece.

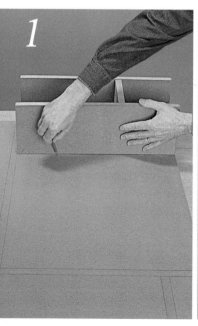

Measure and draw a 6 in.-wide x 3 in.-high box at the bottom of the back piece, centrally between the positions of the two innermost uprights. Shade this area for cutting out. The hole will accommodate the computer and monitor cables that need to be plugged into the wall.

Use a jigsaw to cut off the rounded corners that you marked out in step 2 and the access hole for the computer/monitor cables marked out in step 3. As you cut with the jigsaw, move the back piece around on the workbench to facilitate cutting curves.

5 Take the top shelf piece and place it on the workbench. Mark the positions of the three interior uprights on the uppermost side of the top shelf, following the guidelines given in step 1. Next, mark the angle of cut for the cutaway area at the front of the top shelf. Draw a line between the positions of the front edges of the two innermost uprights. Cut out along this line.

6 Take the left-hand bottom shelf and mark out its position on the two left-hand uprights (as shown), following the guidelines marked against the back piece in step 1. Repeat the process with the two small side shelves positioned between the two right-hand uprights. These should be spaced 6 in. apart from one another on the uprights, and each one should be the same distance from the top shelf and bottom of the unit.

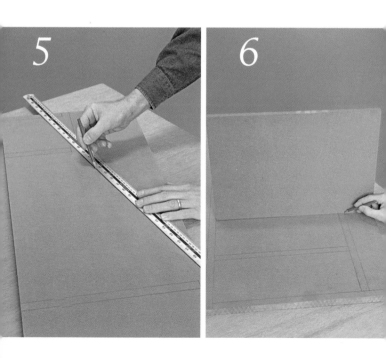

7 Take the marked-out back piece of the unit. Measure
out the positions of clearance screw holes for the six
uprights to be attached to the back piece. Using a ⅛ in.
drill-bit, drill five evenly spaced clearance holes for each
upright into the inside of the back piece, starting 2 in.
in from the positions marked for their ends. Use a piece
of scrap wood under the MDF board when drilling, to
prevent making unwanted holes in your workbench. Be
sure that all your clearance holes are drilled straight
and vertical.

8 Turn the back piece over and countersink the clearance
holes you drilled in step 7 in order to recess the screw
heads. You must always countersink MDF board as
there is no "give" in it.

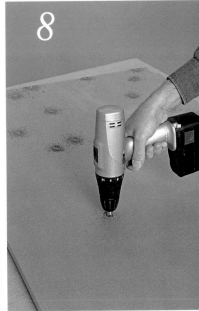

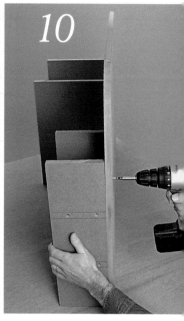

9 Using a combination square and pencil, transfer the guidelines marked on the uppermost side of the top shelf (made in step 5) accurately onto the underside of the shelf. Begin by running the lines down the back edge of the shelf, as shown, and then carefully transfer the lines onto the back of the piece, ensuring your lines are absolutely straight and square to the original guidelines drawn on the top of the shelf.

10 Drill reciprocal pilot holes in the back edges of the shelf uprights, using a ⅛ in. drill-bit, by holding the pieces in position against the back pieces and then drilling through the clearance holes in the backboard that you drilled in step 7. Secure the uprights to the backboard using wood glue and No. 6 (1½ in.) screws. You might find it easier to clamp the pieces to the workbench.

11 Fix the top shelf to the uprights and the back using the same process as described in step 10. Ensure that everything lines up correctly, your holes are straight to one another, and that you do not burst through the sides of the uprights with the drill-bit.

12 Attach the bottom left-hand shelf to its upright central divider, using the same method as described in step 10.

Helpful hints

"Clearance holes" are the wider holes that you drill through MDF to slide the screw through before it bores into the smaller, reciprocal "pilot holes" on the piece to be attached.

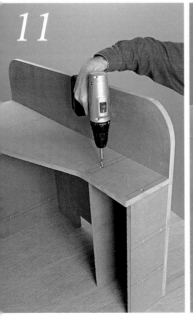

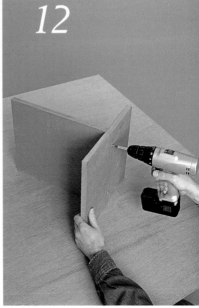

13 Repeat the process described in step 12 with the two small side shelves, aligning them with the positional marks that you made on the two right-hand uprights in step 6. If all your measurements have been absolutely correct, the side shelves should simply slide into place. However, if they are a tight fit, just sand the edges off a little to make them fit comfortably. Then, drill and screw to attach the shelves to both the backboard and the two uprights, following the procedure covered in steps 7–12.

14 Mark the guidelines and positions of the three screw holes to attach the top shelf upright divider. You will need to secure it to the back piece and the top shelf 10 in. from the left-hand edge of the top shelf. Ensure that your guidelines are straight and the divider will fix both vertically and square-on to the back piece and the shelf.

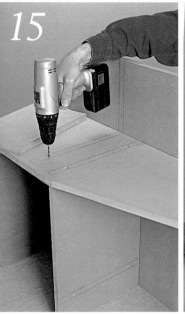 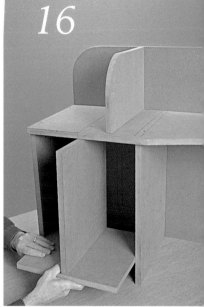

5 Drill the three clearance holes and reciprocal pilot holes required to attach the top shelf upright divider to the top shelf. Do this from the top of the unit, drilling through the top shelf.

6 Secure the top shelf upright divider to the unit using No. 6 (1½ in.) screws and wood glue, as before. Finally, slide the bottom left-hand shelf and its attached central upright divider into position. Drill clearance and reciprocal pilot holes and secure it to the unit using the same method as described in steps 10–13. Fill, sand, and paint the unit as you wish.

chapter 3
The desk

1. Making a magazine organizer
2. Making a desk tidy
3. Making a mail box
4. Making a printer/CPU trolley
5. Building a computer desk

making a
magazine organizer

Paper can be a problem in the office, even in this era of electronic communication. Magazines, catalogs, and brochures all accumulate in no time at all, and there is never enough space to tuck them all away. This wooden rack is a neat and economic paper storage solution that is easy to construct and will fit on a desktop or home office unit, allowing you easy access when you need it. Paint it whatever color suits your taste or your home office furnishings.

Materials

Bottom: 1 piece of MDF ½ x 17 x 10 in.

Back: 1 piece of MDF ½ x 17 x 13 in.

Sides: 2 pieces of MDF ½ x 13 x 11 in.

Dividers: 2 pieces of MDF ½ x 12½ x 10½ in.

Front: 1 piece of MDF ½ x 17 x 2¼ in.

No. 6 (1½ in.) screws • Panel pins • Wood glue

Tools

Workbench • Jigsaw • Tape measure • Rule • Combination square • Carpenter's pencil • Power drill with screw, countersinking, ½ in., ⅛ in., and ⅛ in. bits • Hammer • Abrasive paper/sanding block

Skill level

Intermediate

Time

4 hours

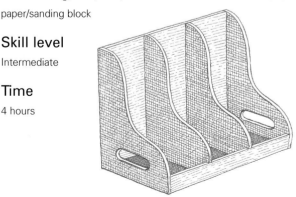

1 Using the photograph on page 71 as a guide, draw the shapes of the dividers and sides onto the four respective MDF pieces. Ensure that you draw the shapes to a size that is big enough to hold a standard magazine. Test by holding a magazine to your final template. To draw smooth curves, use the edge of a small dinner plate and mark around with a pencil. When the design has been fully transferred to the side and divider pieces, shade the areas of waste wood to be cut away.

2 Pin the two side pieces together using a hammer and panel pins. It is important that you pin only through the shaded waste areas and not through the main wood. Repeat the process for the two section dividers. This technique makes it easier to cut two pieces to an identical size.

3 Take the two side pieces, firmly pinned together, and clamp them to the workbench. Select a ½ in. drill-bit to drill a hole large enough to insert a jigsaw blade. Drill a hole in the shaded area of wood that marks out the positions of the handles in the sides of the unit. Take care not to break the pencil line marking the outline of the handles—any rough edges on the waste-wood side of the line can be sanded away after cutting.

4 Insert the jigsaw blade into the drilled hole and begin cutting out the side piece handles. Keep the pieces clamped to the workbench throughout this process and take your time to make an even, smooth cut around the handle shape. Next, use the jigsaw in the same way to cut out the curving front edge of the side pieces. Repeat the process with the two pinned divider pieces.

5 Sand off all cut lines thoroughly. Next, hold the back piece up to one of the side pieces and mark fixing guidelines on it in pencil, ensuring that the back and bottom edges of the side piece are squarely aligned with those of the back piece before marking the pencil lines. Repeat the process with the other side piece.

6 Mark three evenly spaced clearance holes on the bottom outside edge of the side piece in the center of the fixing guidelines that you marked in step 5. Mark four holes in the same way along the vertical edge of the side piece. Drill the clearance holes using a ⅛ in. drill-bit. Place a piece of scrap wood beneath the side piece as you drill. Repeat the process with the other side piece. In the same way, mark and drill fixing positions for the bottom and front pieces.

7 Drill reciprocal pilot holes into the back piece through the clearance holes you drilled in the side pieces in step 6. Hold the two dividers up to the back piece and repeat the process described in steps 5 and 6. Carefully measure to ensure that the two dividers are equally spaced along the width of the back piece. Use a combination square to check that everything is square before finalizing your joints. Use wood glue sparingly and No. 6 (1½ in.) screws to attach the side pieces to the back piece. Repeat the process to attach the dividers and back piece to the rest of the unit.

8 Finally, glue and screw the front piece into position using the same method as described in steps 5–7. Sand, fill, and paint or varnish the unit as you wish.

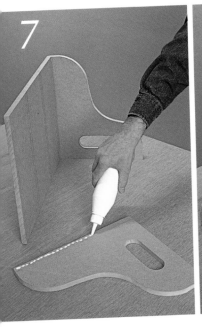

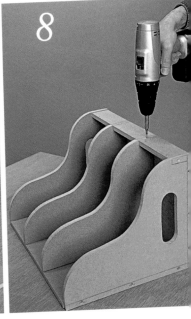

making a
desk tidy

Home offices can become even more cluttered than conventional ones, because often they have to accommodate a lot of personal stuff as well as everyday office materials. This neat little desk tidy offers a practical solution to small storage problems and will help keep your desk and personal space in order. Inexpensive and easy to make, it is an adaptable unit that would look good and come in handy not only in the office but also in just about any other room in the house.

Materials

Sides: 2 pieces of MDF ½ x 10 x 10 in.
Shelves: 3 pieces of MDF ½ x 14 x 10 in.
Tray tops: 2 pieces of MDF ½ x 14 x 2 in.
Top shelf upright dividers: 1 piece of MDF ¼ x 10 x 1½ in.; 1 piece of MDF ¼ x 9 x 1½ in.
No. 6 (1½ in.) screws • Panel pins • Wood glue

Tools

Workbench • Jigsaw • Tape measure • Combination square • Carpenter's pencil • Power drill with pilot hole, screw, countersinking, ½ in., ⅛ in., and ⅛ in. bits • Hammer • Rule • Medium/fine grade abrasive paper/sanding block

Skill level

Intermediate

Time

4 hours

Easy home improvements

1. Measure and cut out all the pieces to the dimensions given in the list of materials. Mark out the positions of the two handle holes and the two feet recesses on one of the side pieces. The handle holes should measure 6 in. across and 1½ in. deep, with rounded-off ends. They should be positioned centrally on the width of the sides and 3 in. down from the top edge of each side piece. Pin the two sides together, with the markings facing upward, ready for cutting out the handle holes and feet recesses, being careful to hammer the pins only through the excess wood that will be cut out.

2. Use a ½ in. drill-bit to drill a hole large enough to accommodate the blade of a jigsaw, with which to cut out the handle holes.

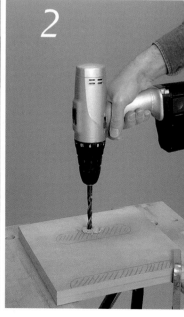

 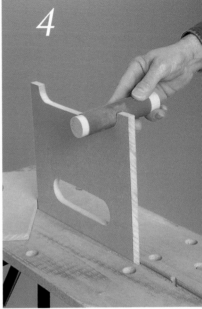

3 Cut out the handle holes from the two pinned side pieces, using a jigsaw. Move the pieces around on the work bench to facilitate your cutting. It is easier to cut a curve with a jigsaw by moving the wood around periodically. Sand off any rough edges or splinters once you have finished cutting out the handle holes.

4 Cut out the feet recesses in the bottom of the two side pieces using the same method as described in steps 2 and 3. The two feet recesses should be positioned centrally 1 in. in from each edge of the side pieces, measuring 1 in. deep with a rounded-off curve at each end. Again, sand off the cut edges to a smooth finish, using abrasive paper wrapped around an offcut piece of dowel or a round tool handle.

5 Mark out the positions of the shelves on both side
pieces. The bottom shelf should be positioned 1½ in.
up from the bottom of the side pieces. The middle
shelf should be positioned 3 in. up from the bottom
shelf. The top shelf should be positioned 3 in. up from
the middle shelf. Transfer the marks accurately from
one side to another so that they are in exactly the
same positions on both sides.

6 Using a ⅛ in. drill-bit, drill nine evenly spaced clearance
holes into each side for the fixing screws for the
shelves—three for each end of every shelf. Use a piece
of old scrap plyboard under the pieces to prevent
making holes in your workbench, and keep the drill
upright as you make the holes.

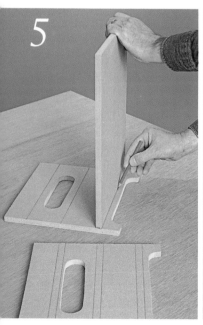

7 Use your power drill to countersink the clearance holes from the outsides of the two side pieces. This will ensure that the screw heads will all be properly recessed in the unit.

8 Hold each of the two side pieces square against each of the three shelves in turn and drill pilot holes into them through the clearance holes in the sides. Drill eighteen ⅛ in. pilot holes in total, three into each end of every shelf. Be sure to keep your drill straight as you drill, so as not to burst through the sides of the shelves with the drill-bit. You might find it easier to clamp the pieces into the workbench as you drill the pilot holes.

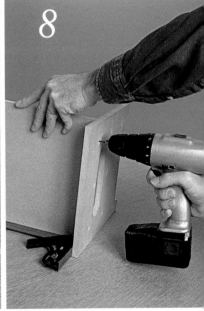

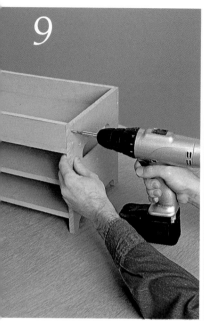

Use your power drill and No. 6 (1½ in.) screws to attach one of the sides to the three shelves. Fix the second side to the shelves using the same method. Next, take the front and back top tray pieces. Use your drill and two screws at each end to attach them square-on to the tops of the side pieces.

Take one of the pieces of ¼ in. MDF that make up the two top shelf upright dividers. Hold it up across the width of the unit. With a pencil, mark the length of cut on the piece of MDF for the shorter of the two upright dividers. Repeat the process for the longer divider, this time positioning the MDF piece along the length of the unit to mark the line of cut.

1 Cut the divider pieces to fit and pin and glue them together on a flat surface with the end of the receiving piece butted up to a backstop clamped to the workbench. This will prevent the pieces from moving as you attach them to one another. The longer divider piece should be positioned 3 in. in from the end of the shorter, cross-dividing piece.

2 Fix the joined upright divider pieces into the unit with a hammer and panel pins, using a piece of scrap wood to butt one end of the longer piece as you nail down on its opposite end. Fill, sand, and paint the unit as you wish.

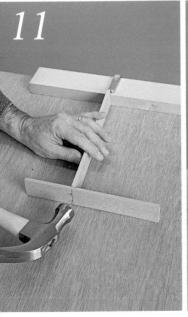

making a **mail box**

This project incorporates nine different "pigeon-holes," to enable the busiest home office worker to sort out their mail. Neat and attractive, the unit will sit comfortably on a desk or filing cabinet and offers a useful adjunct to an orthodox "in/out" tray or filing system. The unit is easy to make and looks good in bare wood. Be sure to make sound, tight joints throughout the unit to ensure that it is level and square all over.

Materials (all lumber is softwood unless otherwise stated)
Top: 1 piece of Parana pine ¾ x 8 x 16½ in.
Bottom: 1 piece of Parana pine ¾ x 8 x 16½ in.
Sides: 2 pieces of Parana pine ¾ x 8 x 18 in.
Shelves: 2 pieces of Parana pine ¾ x 7½ x 16½ in.
Dividers: 2 pieces of Parana pine ¾ x 7½ x 16½ in.
2 mirror-style fixing brackets • No. 8 (1½ in.) screws • Wood glue

Tools
Workbench • Tenon saw • ½ in. chisel • Tape measure • Rule • Combination square • Carpenter's pencil • Power drill with screw, countersinking, ⅛ in., and ⅛ in. bits • Abrasive paper/sanding block

Skill level
Intermediate

Time
4 hours

1 Take the two shelves. Hold them tightly together across the end of one of the upright divider pieces. Mark a fine line across the upright. This gives the measurement of the width of the two shelves, or cross dividers. The remaining length of the upright should then be divided by three. Rub out the original mark at the end of your upright and make two new ones, equidistant along the length of the upright to mark the position of the slots for the cross dividers. Repeat the process with the other upright divider.

2 Mark the positions of the slots to connect the upright dividers and shelves, on all four pieces. Use a combination square to ensure that the joints will be parallel with each other. Mark each slot to half the board's depth. Shade the sections or slots to be removed. Using a steel edge and a sharp craft knife, score out the edges of the slots.

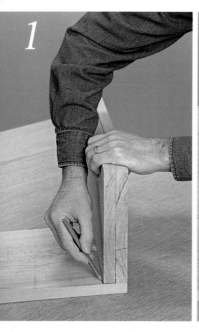

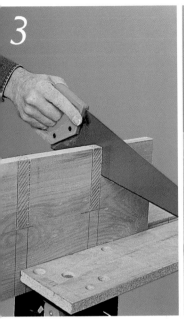

3   Clamp each of the dividers in turn into the workbench.
Be sure to clamp the pieces perfectly upright each time,
as any variations will cause the cuts to be inaccurate.
Use a tenon saw to begin cutting the two slots into each
divider piece, carefully following the guides that you
marked and scored in step 2. Take your time. As you
saw, check frequently that you are staying true to the
score marks. Be careful not to over-shoot the centerpoint
of each piece, as this would leave marks in the wood.

4   Use a sharpened ½ in. chisel and wooden mallet to
remove the waste wood from the slots. Place a piece
of scrap wood underneath the dividers to protect your
workbench. Remove only small sections of waste wood
at a time by chipping away with the chisel and mallet.

5 To finish off each divider slot, put away the mallet and use the chisel by hand to chip gently away from the score lines. This technique is known as "paring." Be sure that all the finished slots have neat, smooth, and above all, square edges. Always chisel in a direction away from the main wood and into the waste wood. This will ensure far neater edges and less finishing work will be required as a result.

6 Once the slots for the two upright divider pieces and two shelves have been cut and chiselled out, use coarse abrasive paper and a sanding block to smooth off any rough edges. Slot the dividers and shelves together to check their fit and alignment. This is the time to make any adjustments to the slots if their fit is too tight. Sand the slots until they fit easily together.

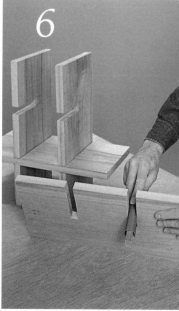

7 Assemble the two upright dividers and shelves by pressing their slots into one another. Hold one of the side pieces alongside the assembled divider pieces. Be sure that the side piece sits square to the shelves and mark their fixing positions onto it using a combination square and pencil. Repeat this process to mark out the other side piece. Allow for the thickness of the top and bottom pieces when marking out each side piece, as the top and bottom of the unit will be attached to its sides. Mark out the top and bottom pieces in the same fashion.

8 Once fixing guidelines have been fully marked out on the two side pieces and the top and bottom pieces, measure and mark the positions of clearance screw holes for fixing. Drill three evenly spaced clearance holes for each joint in the side, top, and bottom pieces.

9   Lightly countersink all the clearance holes so that the heads of all the screws will be fully recessed once the unit is complete.

10   Hold each of the side pieces and top and bottom pieces in position against the divider pieces in turn and drill reciprocal pilot holes into the dividers through the clearance holes you drilled in step 8. Use a ⅛ in. drill-bit. Next, use No. 8 (1½ in.) screws to attach the top, bottom, and side pieces to the dividers. Use a hand-held screwdriver to drive the screws firmly into each hole. Check frequently that the unit is completely square as you are screwing it together. Ensure that on the back side of the frame the side pieces are perfectly flush and that at the front of the unit they slightly overhang. The backs must be flush in order for the mail box to be secured to the wall.

1   Once the unit is fully assembled and you are satisfied with all the joints, sand it down thoroughly to remove any rough edges or pencil marks. Use wire wool (as shown) to bring the wood to a really smooth finish. Finally, wax and polish the entire unit to bring the best out of the wood.

2   When the mail box is complete and polished to your satisfaction, turn it over on the workbench and attach brackets to the back of the unit to secure it to the wall. These should be fitted to hang from the top edge into the top partition, in order to hide them from view when the mail box is fitted to the wall.

making a
printer/CPU trolley

Computers are now an integral part of all our office working lives. But while your desk is bound to have room for your monitor and keyboard, finding space for your printer or computer's power unit is sometimes a problem. This handy printer/CPU trolley can solve that problem, at a fraction of the cost of buying one from a furniture or office supplies store.

Materials

Base: 1 piece of MDF ¾ x 18 x 14½ in.
Top: 1 piece of MDF ¾ x 18 x 14½ in.
Sides: 2 pieces of MDF ¾ x 26 x 15¼ in.
Back: 1 piece of MDF ¾ x 26 x 18 in.
Central upright divider: 1 piece of MDF ¾ x 22½ x 14¼ in.
Shelves: 2 pieces of MDF ¾ x 13½ x 7 in.
No. 6 (1½ in.) screws • Wood glue • 4 x 2½-in. deep castors

Tools

Workbench • Jigsaw • Tape measure • Rule • Combination square • Carpenter's pencil • Power drill with pilot hole, screw, countersinking, ½ in., and ¼ in. bits • Abrasive paper/ sanding block

Skill level

Advanced

Time

8 hours

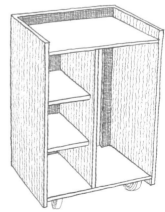

1 Lay the back panel down on the workbench. Place the bottom piece 2 in. in from the bottom edge of the back piece and mark its fixing position by drawing along both its edges. Now position the upright divider centrally along the length of the back panel and mark its position, drawing a line along both its edges. Place the shelves (as shown), and mark their positions 10 in. and 17 in. from the top of the back panel. Draw along both sets of edges.

2 Place your CPU back-end down on the back panel on the line marking the top edge of the bottom shelf and draw around it. You will need to cut a hole out of the back piece to accommodate wires and cables. Measure the hole to fit the size of your particular CPU and the sitings of its various cables and power-points.

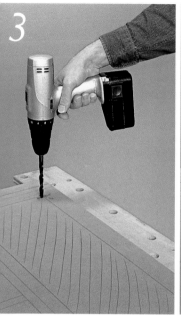

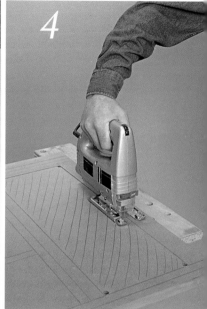

3 Shade with a pencil the area on the back panel to be cut out behind the CPU. Drill four ½ in. holes, one at each corner of the area to be cut out. These must be wide enough to accommodate the blade of the jigsaw that you will use to cut out the hole.

4 Use a jigsaw to cut out the hole in the back panel. Take your time when cutting, moving the backboard around on the workbench to facilitate cutting it out. Be careful not to cut into the workbench. When the hole is cut out, smooth off any rough edges and splinters using abrasive paper.

5   Mark out the two sides of the trolley in the same way
    that you marked out the back panel in step 1. Hold the
    sides of the unit up to the back piece in turn, to transfer
    the lines for the top, base, and shelves in the correct
    positions. Use a combination square to ensure that your
    lines are both straight and square to one another.

6   Next, take the upright central divider piece and mark this
    out against the back panel in the same way as for the
    side pieces in step 5, transferring the guidelines for the
    shelves and other pieces onto the central upright divider.
    Again, use the combination square as you draw your
    lines. The same process then needs to be completed for
    the base and top of the unit, so that all the pieces are
    marked out with the positions of their adjoining sections
    before you begin assembling the unit.

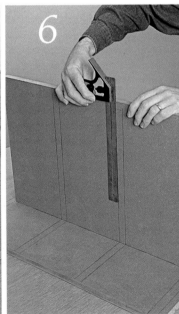

7   Once you have completed the marking-out process, mark evenly spaced points to drill clearance holes in the rear of the back panel for all the screws at the very centers of your fixing guidelines. All clearance and pilot holes in the unit should be sited at least the length of the screws (No. 6 1½ in.) apart from one another, so that the screws do not clash with one another as you assemble the unit. Repeat the process for all pieces of the unit. Be careful to drill the holes straight, to ensure accurate fixings later on.

8   Countersink the clearance holes for all the screw heads being inserted from the exterior of the unit, so that they will be fully recessed once the cabinet has been assembled.

 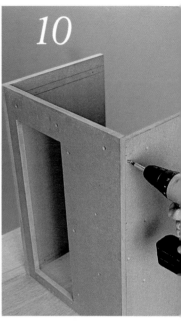

9 Hold one of the side pieces up against the back panel. Hold the pieces against each other in the position they will be in when they have been fixed together. Drill reciprocal pilot holes into the edges of the back panel, through each of the clearance holes that you drilled in the outside of the side pieces in step 7. Be sure that your pilot holes are all drilled accurately and in line with the clearance holes, so that your joints will be as tight and true as possible once the unit has been assembled.

10 Begin assembling the unit by first attaching the two sides to the back panel. Hold the pieces firmly and squarely against each other, ensuring that all fixing guidelines and clearance/pilot holes line up correctly with one another. You will find this easier if you ask someone to help you hold the pieces in position against one another as you screw them together.

1 When you have attached the two sides to the back panel, the next stage is to attach the shelves to the upright central divider. Use the same method as described in steps 9 and 10, holding the pieces together and drilling reciprocal pilot holes for all the screws before fixing the pieces together. Then, offer up the attached divider and shelves (as shown), and fix them with screws to the back and sides of the unit.

2 Complete the assembly of the unit by attaching the top and base pieces to the back panel, sides, and upright central divider. Again, use the same method as explained in steps 9–11, drilling accurate pilot holes through your exterior clearance holes to receive the screws. Attach castors to all four corners of the bottom of the unit. Fill all the countersunk screw holes and any gaps, and then sand and paint the unit as you wish.

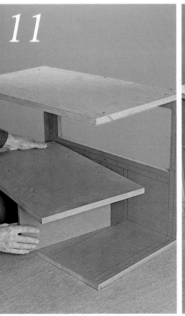

building a
computer desk

A desk is the focal point of any office—a multi-purpose work unit that is often a very personal choice for the user and needs to fulfill a wide range of different requirements. Making your own desktop can overcome many of the hurdles to be encountered in selecting the right work surface, not least because you can adapt its dimensions to the space available and make sure that it is the correct height for you.

Materials (all lumber is softwood unless otherwise stated)

Top: 1 piece of MDF ¾ x 25 x 48 in.
Sides: 2 pieces of MDF ¾ x 28 x 30 in.
Back braces: 2 pieces of MDF ¾ x 6 x 48 in.
Drawer: 1 piece of MDF ¾ x 20 x 23 in.
Drawer runners: 2 x 1 x 13 in. PAR lumber
Drawer backstop: 1 x 1 x 22 in. PAR lumber
Desktop edging: 1 piece of MDF ¾ x 2½ x 48 in.
No. 6 (1 in.) screws • No. 8 (2 in.) screws • Panel pins • Wood glue

Tools

Workbench • Tape measure • Combination square • Carpenter's pencil • Power drill with pilot hole, screw, countersinking, and ¼-in. bits • Hammer • Rule

Skill level

Intermediate

Time

4 hours

Easy home improvements

1 Measure and cut all the pieces of the desk to the dimensions given in the list of materials. Take the piece that will make up the keyboard drawer (¾ in. MDF board measuring 23 × 20 in.) and sand off the long edges thoroughly.

2 Decide which end of the finished desk you would like your keyboard drawer and place it on the underside of the desktop piece, 5 in. in from the end that you have chosen. Align the front edge of the drawer precisely with the front edge of the desktop. Ensure that the pieces are absolutely square with one another, as the drawer will not slide smoothly in its runners if the pieces are not juxtaposed correctly. Draw along the sides of the drawer to mark the precise positions of the keyboard drawer runners on the desktop.

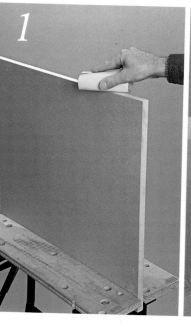

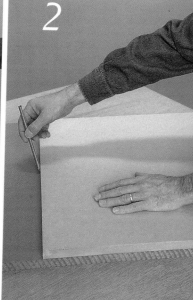

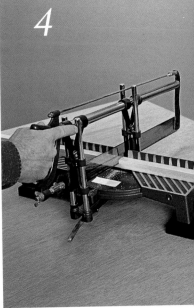

3 Slide the drawer piece forward in line with the marks that you made in step 2, so that its front edge protrudes 10 in. out from the front edge of the desktop. Next, draw a pencil line across the back edge of the extended drawer. This marks the position of the retaining backstop piece that will prevent the drawer from sliding all the way out. The 13 in. un-extended length of the drawer piece that remains positioned over the desktop corresponds with the length that the drawer runners need to be cut to fit.

4 Cut the keyboard drawer runners to length (13 in.) out of 1 x 1 in. PAR timber, using a miter saw. Ensure that your cut lines are absolutely straight and that the ends of the runners are properly squared-up. Smooth off the cut lines with fine-grade abrasive paper.

5 Place the drawer runners in position alongside the drawer, leaving it in its extended position. Slide a piece of thin card between each of the drawer runners and the drawer edges to ensure that there will be a slight tolerance between the pieces that enables the drawer to slide easily in and out. Drill evenly spaced pilot holes to attach the drawer runners to the underside of the desktop with No. 6 (1 in.) screws.

6 Glue sparingly along the bottoms of the two drawer runners, where they will attach to the underside of the desktop. Carefully position them, keeping the spacing card in place. Attach the runners to the desktop with screws through the pilot holes that you drilled in step 5.

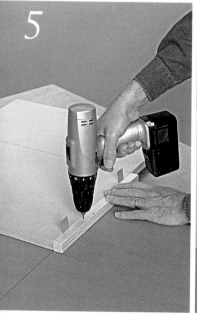

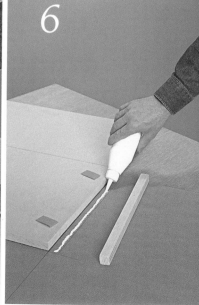

7 Measure and cut out the drawer-retaining pieces from 2 x 1 in. PAR timber. These should be cut to the same length as the drawer runners (13 in.). Position them over the drawer runners and mark three evenly spaced points for screw holes to attach them to the drawer runners. Drill pilot holes, glue, and attach the retaining pieces in position aligned accurately with the drawer runners.

8 Cut the keyboard drawer backstop to fit across the combined width of the back edge of the drawer and the two drawer runners (22 in.). Sand off any rough edges. Clamp the keyboard drawer into the workbench with the back edge facing upward. Hold the backstop in position centrally on top of the back edge of the drawer. Mark and drill three evenly spaced pilot holes and attach the backstop using glue and No. 6 (1 in.) screws.

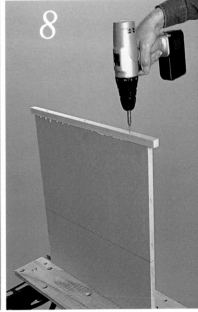

9 Next you need to mark where to attach the desktop and the two back braces to the side pieces. Begin with the desktop. Lay one side piece down and place the desktop 1 in. in from the short edge. Draw a line down both edges of the desktop. Repeat this process on the second side piece. Next, position and mark the back braces. The upper back brace should be positioned flush with the top and side edges of the side pieces (as shown), the bottom one 3 in. up from the bottom edges of the sides and flush with their back edges. Ensure that all your joints are square and true before you draw your pencil guidelines onto the side pieces.

10 Use a cup or saucer and pencil to draw rounded-off corners on the top corners of the two side pieces. Saw and then sand the top corners until they are smoothly rounded off.

1 Cut two 1 x 1 in. battens to a length of 24 in. This corresponds with the depth of the desktop. The battens will be positioned on the side pieces to help support the desktop. Hold the battens against the side pieces and mark their positions, beneath the pencil guidelines for the desktop and just in front of the guidelines for the top back brace. Drill three evenly spaced pilot holes through each batten and into the corresponding side piece. Attach the battens to the side pieces using a little glue and No. 6 (1½ in.) wood screws.

2 Mark and drill seven evenly spaced pilot holes in the side pieces, inside the markings that you made in step 9, in order to attach the desktop and two back braces. Next, turn the sides over and countersink all the holes from the other side.

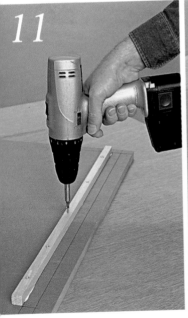

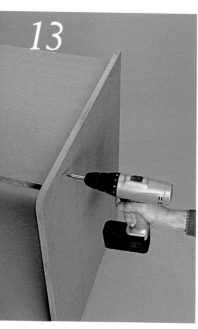

13   Begin assembling the parts of the desk. Hold the desktop and back braces in position against the two side pieces and drill pilot holes into them, through the countersunk screw holes that you drilled into the side pieces in step 12. Use glue and No. 8 (2 in.) screws to secure the side pieces to the desktop. Next, slide the keyboard drawer into position from the back of the unit before attaching the two back braces.

14   Glue and screw the two back braces into position using the same method as described in step 13. Be sure that your joints make a tight, square fit before tightening the screws. Wipe off any excess glue with a damp cloth, as it will squeeze out of the joints and onto the unit as you tighten the screws.

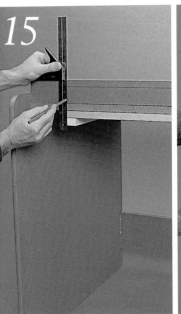

5   Cut out an MDF "lip" to attach to the front edge of the desk. This should be the same width as the desktop (48 in.) and 2½ in. deep. Using a combination square and pencil, draw two vertical lines onto the lip at positions in line with the outside edges of the keyboard drawer. Then, ¾ in. down from the top edge of the lip, draw a horizontal line between the two vertical lines. Cut the lip into four pieces, along the lines you have just drawn.

6   Hold each of the front edge "lip" pieces up to the desk in turn and mark evenly spaced panel pin holes to attach them. Glue and pin the four lip pieces to the front of the desk. You will find it easier to pin the MDF pieces to the front and the drawer if you hammer the pins well into the lip pieces before finally securing them.

glossary

Batten—a narrow strip of wood, often used to describe such a strip used as a support for other pieces

Bevel—any angle other than a right angle at which two surfaces meet

Butt joint—a simple joint where two pieces of wood meet with no interlocking parts cut in them

Clearance hole—a hole drilled to the width of the screw shank, through which a screw passes before entering a pilot hole (*cf.*)

Countersink—to cut, usually drill, a hole that allows the head of a screw, nail, or pin to lie below the surface

Hardwood—wood cut from trees like oak, cherry, and elm, belonging to the botanical group *Angiospermae*

MDF—medium-density fiber-board; a prefabricated material that can be worked like wood

Miter—a joint made by cutting equal angles, usually at 45 degrees to form a right angle in two pieces of wood; cutting such a joint

PAR—"planed all round;" timber that has been planed smooth on all sides

Pilot hole—a small-diameter hole drilled into wood to act as a guide for a screw thread

Rebate—a stepped, usually rectangular, recess, cut along the edge of a piece of wood as part of a joint

Ripping—sawing wood along the grain

Softwood—wood cut from trees like pine, maple, and cedar, belonging to the botanical group *Gymnospermae*

Stencil—a transferable ink or paint pattern

Template—a cut-out pattern on paper or cardboard, used to help shape wood or transfer a pattern (*cf.* stencil)

Upright—a vertical piece of wood, usually part of a frame

index

blind, Venetian 10–15
bolster 19, 21
bookcase 50–57
brackets 10, 12–15, 42, 48–49, 91
bradawl 22, 26,

carpet, laying 16–21
castors 57, 99
chiselling 88
clamping 24–25, 27, 35, 38, 52, 64, 73, 81, 83, 87, 105
combination square 12, 24, 26, 30, 42, 44, 50, 53, 64, 75, 86, 89, 96, 108
computer desk 100–109
CPU/printer trolley 92–99
cross braces 34–39

desk tidy 76–83
desk, computer 100–109
dowel 22, 26–30
drawer
    keyboard 101–103, 105, 108
    runners 102–105
drilling
    clearance holes, 37–38, 45, 54–57, 63–64, 67, 74, 80–81, 89–90, 97–99
    countersinking holes 45, 54, 63, 81, 90, 97, 107–108
    pilot holes 15, 38, 45, 54–55, 64, 67, 75, 81, 90, 97–99, 104–105, 107–108

filling 49, 56

helpful hints 19, 29, 36, 48, 65
hinges, fixing 22, 31

jigsawing, technique 35, 61, 73, 79, 95

keyboard drawer 101–103, 105, 108

magazine organizer 70–75
mail box 84–91
marking out 12, 14, 18, 26, 28, 31, 34–35, 37, 44, 46, 52–55, 60–62, 64, 72, 74, 78, 80, 82, 86, 89, 94–97, 102–103, 106–108
mitering 13, 28, 46–48, 103

office step stool 32–39
organizer, magazine 70–75

pins, panel 14, 32, 34, 72, 73, 78, 83, 109
printer trolley 92–99

runners, drawer 102–105

sanding block 22, 25, 36, 38, 47, 50, 52, 57, 79, 88, 91, 105
screen, home-office 22–31
shelf, book-ended 42–49
shelving unit, desktop 58–67
step stool, office 32–39

tenon saw 22, 24, 32, 35–36,
    42, 50, 52, 55, 87
trolley, CPU/printer 92–99

valance, Venetian blind 10–15

acknowledgments

All photographs taken by Alistair Hughes, except for:

8/9; 40/41; 68/69 Camera Press Ltd.

Illustrations by Stewart Walton.